THE SUBSTANCE OF THINGS HOPED FOR

The Remarkable Women of the Montgomery Bus Boycott and Their Progeny

Estella Conwill Majozo, Ph.D.
Award-Winning Author of *Come Out The Wilderness*

The Substance Of Things Hoped For.
Copyright © 2025 Estella Conwill Majozo
All rights reserved solely by the author. The author guarantees all contents are original and does not infringe upon the legal rights of any other person or work. No part of this book may be reproduced in any form without the permission of the author. The views expressed in this book are not necessarily those of the publisher:

BLACK LEGACY PRESS
WESTCHESTER NEW YORK

BTB PUBLISHING
NEW YORK

ISBN: 978-1-63652-256-2

Printed in the United States of America

Illustrations of women by Henry Gentry.

The Substance Of Things Hoped For

"We who believe in freedom cannot rest
until it comes."
Sweet Honey in the Rock

DEDICATION

To Patrice S. Lowe, my beloved daughter,
Tashara Alexander, my dear daughter-in-law,
and Avery Alexander, my precious granddaughter,
with love.

ACKNOWLEDGEMENT

To Jesus Christ, Our Great Deliverer.

In honor of the women of the Montgomery Bus Boycott who left us a legacy of unity and victory.

And in deep appreciation for the women who participated in this project and inspire others to own their mantles.

ALSO BY THE AUTHOR

Come Out The Wilderness
Libation: A Literary Pilgrimage Through the African American Soul
Shekinah Wellness: Your For the Taking
Jiva Telling Rites
Ringshout: A National Rite of Passage for the New and Promised Generation
Anatomy of the Black Man
To Manifest the Ancestral Dream: 10 Essential Essays
To Manifest the Ancestral Dream: A Play in 5 Acts (Breonna Taylor, George Floyd and Ahmaud Arbery)
The Black Sons of God
Blessings For A New World
The Praise Dancer's Notebook
Women Who Dwell in the Secret Place
Sister Please, Can You Stand a Little Honesty
Freedom Clothes: The Amazing Tale of Thornton and Lucie Blackburn
Freedom Clothes Artifacts: Thornton and Lucie Blackburn Exhibition by Kentucky Artists
Musa and the Slave Ship Angel
This is What I Know About Courage:
Unita Blackwell 1st African American Woman Mayor of Mississippi

The Die-In People: I Can't Breathe!
Middle Passage:105 Days
Blessings for a New World
Love Came Out of the Rain
Grandmother Graces in the Time of Plague
Oh, What a Beautiful Child
Butterfly Blessing in The Face of Cancer
Truth in the Territory

Come On Up To Bright Glory: Testimonies for the New Millennium

CONTENTS

Introduction 8

PART ONE 11
The Bombing 14
Protest 20
Nothing Like Family 25
Commitment 28
Getting Ourselves Born 35
The Challenge 39
Miracle in Montgomery 44
My Own Protest 51
Club From Nowhere 60
Bad Mouthing 63
Barber Shop 66
Revenge 74
How Long? Not Long! 77
Night Whispers 80
Night Watch 83
Mourning 87
When King Was Prince 90
Still Standing 93
Birth 95
The Continuum 104
PART TWO 105

ESTELLA CONWILL MAJOZO

INTRODUCTION

There are many lessons we can take from the historical Montgomery Bus Boycott. Yes, the political striving and push back against the unjust laws and practices of segregation of the day. The endurance of persecution of those who dared to rise up against it. The re-direction and self-reliance of 40,000 people who had previously depended on public transportation. Most striking was the unity, cooperation and faith of an entire Black community that sustained a vibrant protest against injustice for three hundred and eighty-one days.

Most salient in all of this are the contributions that Black women made to the movement.

Rosa Parks, under the auspices of the NAACP, triggered the boycott by refusing to give up her seat on the segregated bus.

The Substance Of Things Hoped For

Jo Ann Robinson spear-headed the protest by distributing to the Black community, along with several from the Women's Political Council, some 40,000 fliers demanding that they stay off the buses.

Georgia Gilmore financed the movement through her 'Hidden Kitchen' that provided money to keep it afloat. Her efforts were so essential that Reverend Dr. Martin Luther King, Jr. said that the boycott would not have been possible without her.

Coretta Scott King was the supportive wife of the man chosen to lead the boycott.

Alberta King gave wise counsel to her son, Reverend King.

Mahalia Jackson lent encouragement through the heartfelt hymns that she sang to Dr. King and the community at large.

Claudette Colvin demonstrated determination even before Rosa Parks, by refusing to submit to the unjust judicial demand to relinquish her seat.

And Mamie Till boldly exposed her son's castrated, lynched body in an open casket before the nation which emboldened the Montgomery community to resist.

Virginia Durr and Jeannie Graetz, two White women, crossed racial boundaries to lend undying support.

These are the women featured in *The Substance of Things Hope For.* Their significant contributions helped to produce and sustain the first and largest demonstration against injustice in U.S. history.

May their cooperation, unity, sense of collective identity and purpose, and their abiding faith in God be an inspiration to you.

The Substance Of Things Hoped For

Part One
The Montgomery Bus Boycott

ESTELLA CONWILL MAJOZO

Rosa Parks
Coretta Scott King
Jo Ann Robinson
Georgia Gilmore
Alberta King
Claudette Colvin
Mamie Till
Mary McLeod Bethune
Mahalia Jackson
Sarah Bradley
Recy Taylor
Virginia Durr
Jeannie Graetz
Sojourner Truth
Harriet Tubman
Wisdom

The Substance Of Things Hoped For

**Mrs. Coretta Scott King.
Wife of Reverend Martin Luther King, Jr.
and Civil Rights Advocate.**

ACT ONE   SCENE ONE

THE BOMBING!

MOMMA GILMORE, ROSA, CLAUDETTE, MAHALIA AND ALBERTA
[SINGS]

Gonna do what the Spirit say do,
Gonna do what the Spirit say do,
What the Spirit say do I'm gonna do, Oh Lord,
Gonna do what the Spirit say do.

Gonna move when the Spirit say move,
Gonna move when the Spirit say move,
When the Spirit say move, I'm gonna move, Oh Lord,
Gonna move when the Spirit say move....
(Freedom Song)

The Substance Of Things Hoped For

[ALL THE CHARACTERS EXIT EXCEPT MOMMA GILMORE.]

MOMMA GILMORE

I'm in my kitchen cooking and Mark busts through the door. "White folks done bombed Reverend King's house! Blowed the front porch clean away!"

"What?!

"A bomb, Momma! Come on!"

He takes off running. When I get there, it looks like all hell done broke loose. Reverend King races from his car. "Coretta!"

Lord, have mercy. Is she in there? Men brandish guns, lift their fists. There is so much noise and confusion.

Reverend King comes back out, trying to fix his mind on what to say.

"If you have weapons, take them home."
What about Miss Coretta?!

"If you do not have weapons, please do not seek them."

They're not trying to hear this. Sister Bertha Mae hollers out, asking about Miss Coretta, and she steps through the mess holding Little Yoki.
[CORETTA ENTERS HOLDING A BABY.]
She looks more mad than petrified and nods for Reverend to go on.

"We must meet violence with non-violence."

Ignorant ass Tyrone nudges me. "Well, Miss Georgia Gilmore, *your* preacher done sure poked the hornet nest this time." He needs to go somewhere with that one tooth hanging out the side of his mouth.

"Brothers and Sisters," Reverend says, "This movement WILL NOT STOP because GOD is with us!" The crowd simmers down to a whisper. They lower their weapons.

And that's the moment, right there, that Reverend became King. He's no longer the outside man local preachers chose to run this boycott that was only supposed to last a day; he's the leader.

One by one, folks drift away. Miss Coretta stands watching.

The Substance Of Things Hoped For

CORETTA

There comes a time when time itself is ready for a change. So help me, Jesus, it's time.

WISDOM
[HOLDS A STAFF OF A LONG STEM PURPLE IRIS.]

Ah, Sister Coretta,
true to your name,
you are the 'little core'
of this movement,
the crux upon which
so much hinges.

My name is Wisdom—
The attendant
at the throne of God.
I was with the Almighty
when He first drew the circle
upon the deep and stretched out
the firmament over it.
I was brought forth and I played,
joyfully before Him.
HA!-llelujah!

ESTELLA CONWILL MAJOZO

And I was sent by the Great I Am
to inspire these sisters of Montgomery
to rise to the greatness
He intends.
[CORETTA EXITS.] [WISDOM EXITS.]

The Substance Of Things Hoped For

**Mrs. Rosa Parks of the NAACP,
who refused to give up her seat on a segregated city
bus to a White man in Montgomery, Alabama, 1955.**

ESTELLA CONWILL MAJOZO

ACT ONE   SCENE TWO

PROTEST

[MOMMA GILMORE TRANSFORMS INTO NARRATOR-ROSA. PUTS ON RED GLOVES.]

NARRATOR ROSA

White folks caused all this, making us pay to get on the bus, then get off, walk to the back, and get back on again. We have to stand when a White person comes and give them our seat. And the meanness of the drivers, pulling off sometimes, just when we get to the back!
 This time I kept my seat, thank you very much.

[ALTERNATE ROSA ENTERS AND SITS CENTER STAGE, PUTS ON SIMILAR RED GLOVES.]

The Substance Of Things Hoped For

The driver came back to me.

"You have to move. White folks need to sit." I pursed my lips, and said—

ALTERNATE ROSA

"NO."

NARRATOR ROSA

Not "I'm sorry, Sir." Not "I'm incapacitated." Just plain old, bare-faced, unapologetic "NO." I folded my hands and looked out the window.

"What you mean, Naw?!" he said fingering his gun. "Your black ass is goin' to jail."

I was anxious—

ALTERNATE ROSA

Who wouldn't be given our history.

NARRATOR ROSA

Plus, drivers were given authority to arrest us.

ALTERNATE ROSA

But I did it anyway.

NARRATOR ROSA

Most salient in my mind was the vicious murder of that child, Emmett Till. But there was something else in that exchange. In the driver's eyes, an unadulterated fear.

ALTERNATE ROSA

What does he have to be afraid of? He's the one with the gun.
[POSES FOR MUG-SHOTS.]

…7053, that's my mug shot number.

NARRATOR ROSA

Somebody said those numbers mean it's going take 70 years and 53 days for us to finally get free.

ALTERNATE ROSA

Lord, please don't let it take that long!

[WISDOM ENTERS.]

NARRATOR ROSA

My husband didn't want me to be the symbol at first. He worked on that Scottsboro case and knew how nasty White folk could be. But he finally agreed. Mr. Nixon of the NAACP and the Durrs bailed me out.

ALTERNATE ROSA

The Durrs will pay for that though because if it's one thing White folk hate is other White folk sticking up for the Colored.

WISDOM

> *Rosa Parks disobeyed the law*
> *just as Queen Esther did*
> *in coming unsummoned before the king.*
> *Can't you see it?*
> *Our Sister Rosa is another Queen Esther.*

ALTERNATE ROSA AND NARRATOR ROSA
[FACE EACH OTHER.]

Another Queen Esther.

WISDOM

"for such a time as this."

[ALTERNATE ROSA AND WISDOM EXIT.]
[NARRATOR REMOVES GLOVES.]

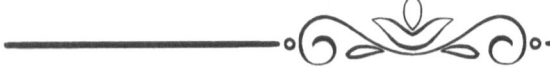

ACT ONE   SCENE THREE

NOTHING LIKE FAMILY

MOMMA GILMORE

The day after the bombing, here comes Daddy King, Reverend's father from Atlanta. You don't have to wonder what they talk about behind closed doors. I've been cooking all day and bring over the food. I'm not trying to stay up in their business—just bring the dinner and leave.

Miss Coretta opens the door—
[CORETTA ENTERS.]
looking like she needs a lot more than caramel cake.

CORETTA

Sister Gilmore. You are a site for sore eyes.

MOMMA GILMORE

Me?! ...We unload food from my car. Daddy King's in the parlor holding a glass of ice-tea in his hand—or ice something.
Miss Alberta, Reverend's momma, is sitting at the end of the mantle. Once we're in the dining room, Miss Coretta opens up.

CORETTA

I've seen White folk madness before, Sister Gilmore. My daddy's lumber mill was burned to the ground after he refused to lend it to a White logger. This bombing is just a reiteration of their hatred. I don't know what Daddy King's in there telling Martin, but we've talked about this. Martin and I are in this boycott all the way, and mark my words, Sister Gilmore, by the grace of God, we will win.
[CORETTA EXITS.]

The Substance Of Things Hoped For

**Mrs. Alberta King,
Mother of Reverend Martin Luther King, Jr.**

ESTELLA CONWILL MAJOZO

ACT ONE   SCENE FOUR

COMMITMENT

MOMMA GILMORE
[SITS ON STOOL, TALKS ON THE TELEPHONE.]

...*How they doing?!"*
Jaunita, Girl, all I can say is they're doing. Daddy King's gonna have plenty to say. I imagine about now he's telling Reverend that he don't have to be bothered with these Redneck Bamas! Might even be telling him that he and Miss Coretta can come back to Atlanta—co-pastor at Ebenezer with him!

He's not for all this foolishness. Reverend King's a Morehouse man! Been all up there in Boston, got his Ph.D.! And you better believe it stands for more than 'Piled Higher and Deeper!' He's smart.

The Substance Of Things Hoped For

... *"Why they push him out front that way?!"*
You know why. These local Negroes have to live with these White folks if things don't work out. He's probably telling him, "You need to think this through, Son. No use putting your and Coretta's life on the line. You said yourself; they called threatening your life if you didn't leave town in three days."

... *"Is that true?!"*
If I'm lying, I'm flying. You don't see no features, do you? Some voice on the phone in the middle of the night say, 'Nigger leave.' Three days later, BOOM!

... *"What I think he gonna do?"*
Lord only knows. His daddy's pretty stiff-hearted about this. Miss Coretta's not standing for any of this though, She's been in the thick of protest long before Reverend. Some mess about how they did her in college,

Reverend King probably looking him dead in the eye by now.

"Daddy, The Lord's doing something different here in Montgomery, something He's never done before."

Miss Alberta is sitting there, bidding her time.

[ALBERTA ENTERS, SITS CENTER STAGE, AND SNAPS OPEN A GOLD FAN.]
[WISDOM ENTERS AFTER HER.]
Far as she's concerned, they can pack their things up now.

[MOMMA GILMORE PANTOMIMES TALKING.]

WISDOM

> *Alberta, listen to me.*
> *You bear the spiritual imprint*
> *of the elder Elizabeth,*
> *mother of John the Baptist,*
> *who beheld the mother*
> *of our King.*
> *You are called to recognize the calling*
> *of the one standing before you,*
> *and to give him your blessing.*

ALBERTA

My blessing?! These ungodly scorpions are trying to kill my son. What am I supposed to do? Let him be a bull's eye for their racism?

WISDOM

Alberta,
The Lord is calling your son to lead.
You brought your son to manhood
now support him in his calling.

ALBERTA

Lord, have mercy.

WISDOM

Trust God. Have faith in Him..

ALBERTA

It's not God that I'm not trusting.

WISDOM

It's not just about them.

ALBERTA

[STANDS.]

...Martin, Son, you're a reverend, called to do a reverend's work. Nobody said it would be easy. If you feel God is calling you to do this, then stand.

I see you over there staring a hole in my head, Daddy, And I know what you're thinking, 'Bunch, he needs to consider his wife and little Yolanda.' But Corrie's in this all the way. Martin's going to do the Lord's bidding. You may as well call Shuttlesworth over in Birmingham, Abernathy, and the rest of them, and start praying him up to be fit for the battle.
[ALBERTA TURNS AND FACES WISDOM DIRECTLY AND NODS HER RECOGNITION.]

WISDOM

>HA-llelujah!
>Bunch is what her husband calls her.
>It is the nickname
>the family has given.
>Everything this woman of God does,
>thinks, or breathes is in bunches.
>
>For her, it is all about family,
>She is the spiritual matriarch.
>They are because she is.

The Substance Of Things Hoped For

As it is written;
Train up a child!
[WISDOM EXITS. ALBERTA EXITS WHILE SINGING UNDER HER BREATH.]

<u>ALBERTA</u>

…Gonna do what the Spirit say do,
Gonna do what the Spirit say do,
What the Spirit say do, I'm gonna do, Oh Lord,
Gonna do what the Spirit say do….

ESTELLA CONWILL MAJOZO

**Mrs. Georgia Gilmore,
Midwife of the Montgomery Movement.**

The Substance Of Things Hoped For

ACT TWO   SCENE 1

GETTING OURSELVES BORN

MOMMA GILMORE
[FOLDS WHITE HAND TOWELS.]

Momma Gilmore is what some of them call me. Miss Georgia Gilmore is what church folks say. Reverend King calls me "Tiny."

All I can say--he'd better be glad he a preacher. Folks around here got better sense than tease about my fat. When they ask me why he calls me that, I tell them it's because he associates me with the little people. I do all the midwifing around these parts.

I got called to Daisey Mae's house the other day. Her water broke and Sylvester, her banjo-plucking, gin-drinking husband, liked to knock the door off the hinges. When we got to their house, she's hollering like she's dying.

Ah, it won't be long now, I tell Slyvester, who's tripping over his own two feet. I'm thinking the man gonna bring some boiling water, or get extra towels, but he goes and starts up the record player on the front porch, like Big Momma Thornton's got the power to drown out the screams.

"Sylvester, Cut that noise down!"

Ordinarily, Jaunita would be with me in the next room, praying or humming borning songs. Not hound-dog, gutbucket, chitlin' circuit blues. That's juke joint. Not the time or the place.

Like I say, the main thing is to be calm and try to calm the momma. Talk softly to her. And call on the Lord.
Then all of a sudden, the baby's out. She takes her first cry, and in an inkling I see the face of God.

...Lord, I get it, I do.
[DANCER ENTERS AND DANCES THROUGHOUT THIS UNDERLINED SECTION.]
Borning is your way of reminding us
You're still blessing.

The Substance Of Things Hoped For

We got to get from one place to another.
That's what this boycott is about, ain't it?
Getting ourselves born.
We may have to push our way through.
We may have to get real bloody,
but whatever we got to go through,
we getting ourselves born.

[DANCER EXITS.]
[WISDOM ENTERS.]

ESTELLA CONWILL MAJOZO

**Mrs. Jo Ann Robinson
posted notices throughout Montgomery, Alabama
calling for a boycott of public transportation.**

ACT TWO   SCENE TWO

THE CHALLENGE

WISDOM

Sister Jo Ann
spent years in the academy
at the feet of the learned,
but never gave a single thought
to the meaning of her family name,
Robinson.
If she had she would have discovered
that it is akin to Ben Rabbi,
meaning son of Rabbi.
She is, indeed, a teacher
at the university,

but on this day, HA-llelujah,
Sister JoAnn Robinson
will marvelously teach
all of Montgomery.

[EXITS.]

JO ANN

[PASSES OUT FLIERS TO AUDIENCE WHILE ANNOUNCING.]

"Stay off the buses!"
"Boycott the buses!"
"If you need a ride, come to the church!"
"Don't ride the bus!"

I stayed up all night making these fliers. My poor arm is cramped from all that cranking. Fifty-two thousand, five hundred cranks! But we're doing this. There's no way I'm letting this harvest pass.

We warned them, the woman's Political Council did, a year ago in a letter to the mayor telling him that if violence didn't stop on the buses–and there was plenty—we would boycott. We were three hundred professional women strong. When we got word that they had arrested Rosa, ah-ha! it was on! We put our saltiness to another use. Twenty of us sprinkled

The Substance Of Things Hoped For

the town with these fliers. We put them on bus stops, telephone poles, the front of groceries, anywhere Colored folks would be.

I don't know how many people showed up the next day where we met. It must've been all of Colored Montgomery.

After Reverend King was elected leader, Mr. Nixon addressed some of the men who were still riding the fence—they could lose their livelihood, wake up in the middle of the night with hooded vigilantes and burning crosses on their front lawns, they could be lynched by morning. But Mr. Nixon didn't care about any of that now.

"What's the matter with you people? Here you have been living off the sweat of these washerwomen all these years and you have never done anything for them. The time has come when you have to learn to be grown men, not scared little boys!"

That splashed cold water in their faces. Right then, one by one, they started to stand.
[STANDS.]
[WISDOM ENTERS.]

And Miss Rosa, who was jailed for not giving up her seat, and I, who stayed up making thousands of fliers, and the women from the council, who posted them all around the

city, scooted over—and that, my dear, is how the men became the bosses of the movement.
[EXITS.]

WISDOM

Sister Jo Ann,
is likened to Mary Magdalene.
Have you ever wondered
why Jesus, Our Lord, chose her
to spread the news of His resurrection?
a woman who was considered
inferior by most men of the day,
who did not hold any position
of prominence as they travelled
from town to town?.

Why choose a woman to tell the news
of the largest, most impactful,
most sacred revolution
on earth?

Think about it.
Why?

[EXITS.]

The Substance Of Things Hoped For

PLEASE STAY OFF OF ALL BUSES ON MONDAY.

ESTELLA CONWILL MAJOZO

ACT TWO   SCENE THREE

MIRACLE IN MONTGOMERY

[CORETTA SIPS HER COFFEE, READS THE PAPER, THEN ANSWERS A KNOCK AT THE DOOR.]

ROSA

I'm on my way to work. Thought you could use some company.

CORETTA

[HUGS ROSA.]
Reverend's already gone. Come on in, have some coffee.

The Substance Of Things Hoped For

[ROSA HANDS HER A CUP OF COFFEE.]

The morning bus should be coming in a few minutes. We can get a good view from this window.
[THEY STAND AT THE FRONT WINDOW.]
I don't know how long this boycott will last but the carpools are ready, seven days a week.

ROSA

Seven. That's the first of my mug shot numbers. **7053.**

I told you, didn't I, that Miss Dimple ran looking for the number's runner as soon as she found them out?

CORETTA

Your people.

ROSA

They get it honestly though. Between our spirituals being codes of escape, our dances before enslavers holding gestures of ridicule, and our quilts flung over backyard fences pointing the way north for runaways, it's no small wonder.

CORETTA

Miss Rosa, you've been playing with those numbers.

ROSA

Seven—our seven-days a week carpool commitment.

CORETTA

Alright now..

ROSA

Zero, our no retaliation policy.

CORETTA

That's good.

ROSA

Five, the number of grace.

CORETTA

We're going to need .plenty of that.

The Substance Of Things Hoped For

ROSA

And three, the number of our demands—
[COUNTS ON HER FINGERS.]
Courtesy on the bus,
Hiring our drivers,
and Honoring a first-come

CORETTA AND ROSA

[LAUGH.]
first-seated policy.

CORETTA

Miss Rosa, look, here come the lights!
[BOTH OF THEM STRETCH TO SEE.]

ROSA

Please be empty, bus!

CORETTA

Please, please.

ROSA

Miss Coretta —

CORETTA

Girl!

CORETTA AND ROSA

There's nobody on the bus!

CORETTA

Lord have mercy Jesus!

All the maids,

ROSA

Gone!

CORETTA

All those cooks who stand on their feet all day long,

ROSA

Gone!

The Substance Of Things Hoped For

CORETTA

Janitors, gardeners, and sanitation workers, who keep the city moving, all of them,

ROSA AND CORETTA

G-O-N-E!

CORETTA

Look, look—they're all together in cars, waving, [WAVE OUT THE WINDOW.]   Hey hey!

[ROSA AND CORETTA SING AND DANCE]
Woke up this morning with my mind
and it was stayed on freedom—
Come on, you know this,
Work up this morning with my mind
and it was stayed on freedom—
Woke up this morning with my mind
and it was stayed on freedom,
Hallelu, Hallelu,
Hallelujah!
(Spiritual)

[CORETTA AND ROSA EXIT.]

ESTELLA CONWILL MAJOZO

Ms. Claudette Colvin,
A fifteen-year-old girl who refused
to give up her seat on a Mongomery bus
and was put into jail.

The Substance Of Things Hoped For

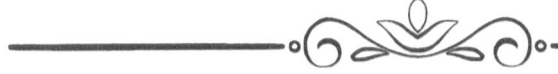

ACT TWO   SCENE FOUR

MY OWN PROTEST

ROSA
[PUTS ON RED GLOVES.]

I'm not the first woman who refused to give up my seat. Three other women did it before me. Aurelia Browder is one of them. Mary Louise Smith is another.

CLAUDETTTE
[ENTERS DONNING AN AFRO AND GLASSES. PUTTING HER HAND ON HER HIP, SHE POSES.]

But I'm the main one.
Miss Claudette 'Get-your-facts-straight!' Colvin.
[SITS CENTER STAGE AND CROSSES HER LEGS.]

ROSA

This fifteen year old held her own protest. Sit there in the Colored section, bottom glued to her seat!

CLAUDETTTE

That girl wasn't gonna sit here. She ain't elderly, on a cane, or limping her last. I don't see no cast on her leg. She the same as me, except for her color and that over-bleached, blond, hanging hair.

ROSA

The police came and asked her why she was sitting there.

CLAUDETTTE

It's my constitutional right. I paid my fare!

ROSA

They wrestled her up,
[CLAUDETTE WRESTLES HERSELF UP.]

put her in the back of a squad car,
charged her with disorderly conduct, and assaulting police officers. They said she clawed and kicked the police.

CLAUDETTE

That's a lie. I'm still breathing, ain't I?
I held my own protest, but ain't no way Colored folks in Montgomery gonna let me be the symbol for the cause. Specially not no NAACP Negroes. 'Uh uh,' they say, 'not with that nappy head, and sassy-mouth!' 'Plus,' they gossip, 'she pregnant by that married man.'
Facts.

That's alright. The Bible woman at the well was berated, too. And she turn around and tell the whole town, "Come see a man."
[WISDOM ENTERS.]

WISDOM

> *"...a man who told me everything*
> *I ever did."*
> *Finish the scripture, Child of God.*
> *Speak the Word in context,*
> *Young Sister*

CLAUDETTE

They color struck. We don't do good together.

They the reason I stop hot combing my hair. To separate myself further from them.

Mr. Tyrone, who gets on everybody's last nerve, got his toothless mouth on me. Him with that tutti-frutti, wanna be 'Little Richard' conk.

The only reason they take the dark skin-did Kings is 'cause they're Kings. Lemon-sucking, highfaluting, hoity-toity Negroes.

[STANDS UP DISGUSTED.]

WISDOM

*Lemon-sucking... high-faluting...
hoity-toity Negroes?*

*Young Sister, Young Sister.
Your family name, Colvin, means black,
coal black.
You are emblematic of the blackness
that challenges the hearts
of the oppressors.
You are rejected by your own fold.
who have internalized
the hatred put upon them.*

The Substance Of Things Hoped For

In their arrogance, they reject the very one pointing the way.

CLAUDETTE

I don't mind they didn't let me be the symbol because I really didn't have much choice in the matter. On the bus that day, it was like Sojourner Truth pushed me down on one shoulder, and Harriet Tubman shoved me down on the other.

[LOOKS OVER SHOULDER TO THE LEFT AS IF LOOKING AT SOJOURNER AND HARRIET, THEN CLOSES HER EYES.]

Ancestors.

ESTELLA CONWILL MAJOZO

**Miss Harriet Tubman,
Conductor of the Underground Railroad.**

The Substance Of Things Hoped For

**Miss Sojourner Truth,
Abolitionist and Women Rights Advocate.**

ESTELLA CONWILL MAJOZO

WISDOM

The Cloud of Witnesses
include your great ancestors,
your mothers who have passed on,
your grandmothers, aunts,
and matriarchs—
all who have submitted
to the will of the Eternal God.

Know that the same God
who aided them
is able to lift you from whatever
burdens you bear.

[ROSA AND CLAUDETTE EXIT.]

The Substance Of Things Hoped For

**Mrs. Georgia Gilmore,
Midwife of the Montgomery Bus Boycott.**

ESTELLA CONWILL MAJOZO

ACT TWO　　　　　　SCENE FIVE

CLUB FROM NOWHERE

MOMMA GILMORE
[COUNTING DOLLAR BILLS.]

I got the idea of fixing food for the rallies—sandwiches, nickel pies—and selling them for the cause. White folk can't see how we're doing it. From my hidden kitchen we make sure Reverend King has money to keep things going. [PUTS CASH IN HER BOSOM AND WINKS.]

We call ourselves "Club From Nowhere"—clever, ain't it?

WISDOM

Well, yes.

The Substance Of Things Hoped For

MOMMA GILMORE

We pull between a hundred twenty-five to two hundred dollars a week. That's good green money. Not White money, Not Colored money. But I like to say, money with a tongue.
[LAUGHS.]
Yeah, Honey, "Money talks" ...and you know the rest.

The boycott has multiplied into months. A hundred days now. Reverend King stopped by the house and said in his deep preacher voice, "You've been bringing meals down to the rallies. Why don't you set up your dining room as a serving place? You could sell dinners right here, and my people can sit and eat securely, without the walls listening. And I won't have to worry if somebody's slipping Ex-lax or something worse in my meal." By the time we finished talking, it's good to go.

WISDOM
[COMES OVER TO MOMMA GILMORE AND EXTENDS PURPLE IRIS TOWARDS HER.]

>   *Your family name, Gilmore,*
>   *bespeaks your mantle.*
>   *"Great servant of the Lord."*
>   *You are in the sacred footsteps*

of the prophet, Mariam,
who assisted her brother, Moses.
Sister Georgia Gilmore, you are
[TOUCHES STAFF ON GILMORE'S SHOULDERS.]
The Midwife of the Movement.

King will say
that without your faith
and your efforts this movement
would not have been possible.
[WISDOM EXITS.]

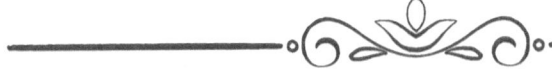

ACT TWO   SCENE SIX

BAD MOUTHING

MOMMA GILMORE

White folks get up early just to bother us when we're walking to work. The weather has warmed up, and they're out like flies.

"Take the bus, fools!" they shout from cars.

"It's raining pitch forks and nigger babies!"

Rebel flags wave out the car windows. But they no more nasty mouth than me. Like I say, I give them *"One for the money, two for the show!"* You know the rest—*"Mess with me, honky, find your UH on the floor!"*

Reverend King tells me about that. "Tiny, your nasty-mouth turns the pure air blue!"
I laughed and said I'll work on it.

Bottom line, we're winning, and they're mad as hornets. Before this boycott, they thought we depend on them to breathe.

Pass them on the street, they walk straight through you. When they're in groups, they're real bold. They losing money, big money, three-thousand dollars a day from us not riding the buses. There's sure enough a hole in the bucket, dear Liza. And they don't know how to fix it.

When they get this riled, they likely to show up in their Klan sheets. Burn a cross in your yard. Drag you from the back of a wagon. Huh, rope you to a tree.

The Substance Of Things Hoped For

**Mrs. Mamie Till-Mobley,
Mother of 14-year-old Emmett Till,
who was murdered in Mississippi in 1955.**

ESTELLA CONWILL MAJOZO

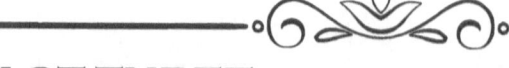

ACT THREE   SCENE ONE

BARBER SHOP

MOMMA GILMORE

Lynch. That's exactly what they did to young Emmett four months before all this started. They castrated, crucified, and drowned him.

My son, Mark, was at Mr. Malden's barber shop. Reverend and other men were there letting off steam. The child buried his face in a magazine and listened.

[SITS, HOLDS MAGAZINE TO FACE, LOWERS IT.] [CHARACTER COME IN ONE BY ONE AND ACT AS MEN IN THE SHOP.]

The Substance Of Things Hoped For

CORETTA

"Reverend King, no offense, but these folk showing their bare behinds."

ROSA

"And some of us still run behind them like their ice is colder!"

CLAUDETTE

"And don't let Miss Ann come through with her 'tresses' bouncing. You best look away, cross-eyed or something. They'll cut you for that."

ALBERTA

"Heck, they 'll do more than cut you. Rope you up and toss your ass down river. You know how they did that boy Emmett Till."

JO ANN

"That's a God-awful shame how they did that boy."

CORETTA

"Yeah, fifteen years old. Uh. Come down from Chicago and they claim 'wolf-whistled' at some White woman."

ROSA

"The Colored man's mortal sin."

CORETTA

"Rednecks come right up to the boy's uncle's house and snatched him out the front door!"

JO ANN

"They would have had to talk to my pistol about that."

CLAUDETTE

"What you talking 'bout, man? They'd murder everybody in the house."

CORETTA

They took his poor body and dumped it in the Tallahatchie. Weighted him down so nobody'd find him. His momma the one decided to have an open casket. Miss Mamie wanted the world to see what they did to her baby.

[WISDOM ENTERS CENTER STAGE. SHE AND CHARACTERS LOOK TO THE BACK, TRANSFIXED.]
[MAMIE WALKS SLOWLY FROM THE BACK DOWN CENTER AISLE, DONNING A BLACK DRESS AND VEIL, EMBRACING A PICTURE OF EMMETT.]

MAMIE TILL

Two months ago, I had a nice apartment in Chicago. I had a good job. I had a son. When something happen to the Negroes in the South, I said, 'That's their business, not mine.'
Now I know how wrong I was.
[WALKS A LITTLE FURTHER.]

The murder of my son has shown me that what happens to any of us in the world had better be the business of us all. God told me, "I have taken one from you, but I will give you thousands."

WISDOM

Look at Sister Mamie's family name, Till.

ESTELLA CONWILL MAJOZO

It means to work the land,
to get it ready for planting
and harvesting. Amen.
That is what her son's death did
for the people of Montgomery.
It broke them wide open
and prepared them for the planting,
Sister Jo Ann wet the ground
for this movement, Amen,
but Sister Mamie's blatant response
to her son's death surely tilled it.
She bears the very contours
of Mary, the mother of Jesus,
whose death redeemed the world,
Amen.

[MAMIE EXITS SLOWLY DOWN THE MIDDLE AISLE.]
[CHARACTERS SLOWLY EXIT.]
[DANCER ENTERS AND DANCES THE UNDERLINED SECTION.]

WISDOM

<u>The question is</u>
<u>what do you do with all that pain?</u>

The Substance Of Things Hoped For

*with death,
disappointment,
 depression,
and depravity?*

*You set it at the feet of God.
You believe that He can
and will give you beauty for ashes—*

*You believe that He will take you
through the dark places and give you,
Ha-llelujah! joy in the morning.*

*You believe with all your heart
that He is a rewarder
of those who love Him and are called
to His good purpose—*

*You believe, Beloved,
that you are in the palms
of His resurrected hands.*

[DANCER EXITS.]
[WISDOM EXITS.]

ESTELLA CONWILL MAJOZO

**Mrs. Virginia Durr,
Supporter of Montgomery Bus Boycott.**

The Substance Of Things Hoped For

**Mrs. Jeannie Graetz,
Supporter of Montgomery Bus Boycott.**

ACT THREE   SCENE TWO

REVENGE

ROSA

[STANDS.]

Didn't I tell you Clifford and Virginia Durr would pay for their involvement? Well, they and another White couple paid dearly. Reverend George Graetz and his wife, Jeannie's, house was dynamited. .

Those who did it meant to send a clear message that they regarded them as traitors. They , thank God, were not in the house with their infant daughter.

She decided to support the boycott as soon as she heard they had arrested me.

Even insisted once on sitting in the Colored section of the theatre. The owners were so scared there would be a riot they ushered them to the general section and offered them free tickets.
[VIRGINA ENTERS.]

VIRGINIA

They call us 'Communist.' 'N' lovers. Some even call of followers of Hitler. But we are not the ones bombing houses. We are not the ones waving Nazi flags from our pick-up trucks.
[VIRGINIA AND ROSA EXIT.]

WISDOM

[ENTERS.]

> *This spiritual striving*
> *is a two-fold in purpose,*
> *break oppression*
> *and transform the hearts*
> *of the oppressors.*
>
> *God does not wish that any should perish*
> *but that all should come*
> *to repentance.*

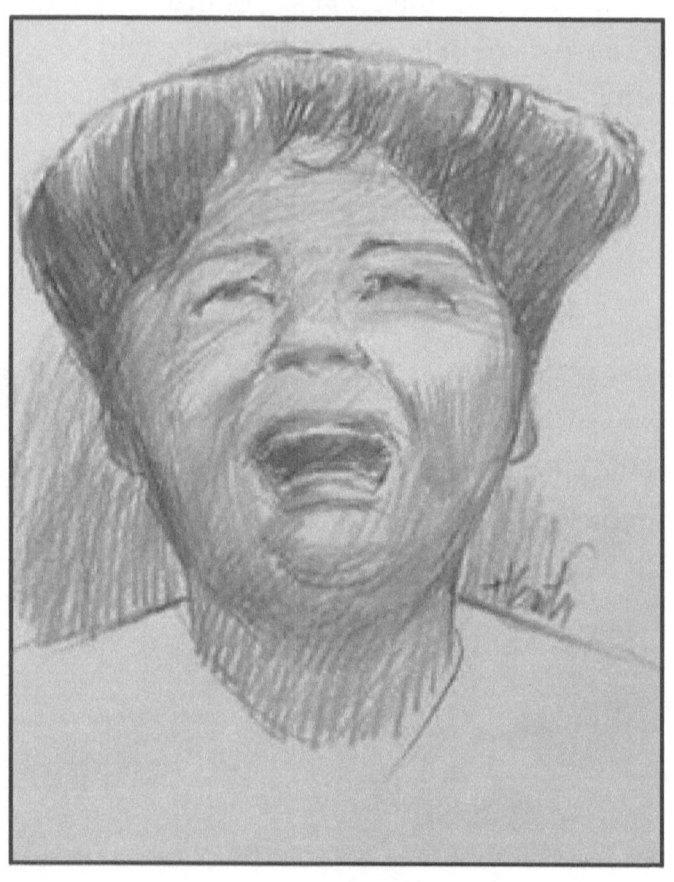

**Mrs. Mahalia Jackson
singing *There is Power in The Blood*.**

ACT FOUR   SCENE ONE

HOW LONG?
NOT LONG

MOMMA GILMORE
[SITS HOLDING A CHURCH FAN.]

We're all here in church. Reverend King has delivered his sermon—"However difficult the moment. It will not be long, because truth, crushed to earth, will rise again." Miss Coretta's eyes are watering. Miss Rosa is just sitting there. Three hundred twenty days is a long time. Miss Mahalia Jackson's with us this morning. Sometime, when Reverend's real low, he calls her and she sings to him.

WISDOM

Like David playing his harp for Saul.

MOMMA GILMORE

"Sing the song, Mahalia," he says, and he means, *"Precious Lord, take my hand."* But this morning, the whole church needs uplifting.

The choir director welcomes Miss Mahalia to sing.

[MAHALIA RISES FROM AUDIENCE HOLDING A CHURCH FAN AND COMES TO CENTER STAGE.

And the song leaves her mouth even before she takes the microphone.

MAHALIA
[ENGAGES AUDIENCE TO SING ALONG. ROSA, MOMMA GILMORE, CLAUDETTE JOIN IN.]

(Chorus)
There is power, power,
    Come on!
Wonder-working power
in the Blood of the Lamb.

Sing along with me!

There is power,
[DANCER DANCES DOWN MIDDLE AISLE.]
Power, Wonder-working power
in the precious Blood of the Lamb.
    Come on up here, Miss Coretta. Sing it with me!

[CORETTA COMES FORWARD AND SINGS.]
*   Would you do service*
*   for Jesus your King?*
There's power in the blood,
Power in the Blood—

[CORETTA]
*   Would you like David*
*   His praises to sing?*
There's wonder-working power
in the Blood.
[ALL CHARACTERS COME BACK TO STAGE.]
There is power, Power, Wonder-working power,
in the Blood of the Lamb.
There is power, Power. Wonder-working power
in the Precious Blood of the Lamb!
    (Lewis E. Jones)

ACT FOUR   SCENE TWO

NIGHT WHISPERS

JO ANN

Sh-h-h, night whispers. Come Monday morning, authorities are going to arrest our drivers for not having the right license to transport people. I suppose you have to have a chauffeur's license, or a taxi license. The scuttlebutt came through the Colored telegram—a maid overhearing White folk's plans as they sipped their bourbon.

On the morning it's supposed to happen, eighty-nine of us show up to the courthouse and turn ourselves in! Television and press all around. Stuck out our wrists and called their bluff! "You want a few of us? Here, take us all!"

The Substance Of Things Hoped For

The police looked foolish. We were released from jail, our true faces cracking up behind our masks. Reverend King addressed the press outside the jail. "I was proud of my crime–the crime of joining my people in non-violent protest against injustice."

Go ahead, Reverend, *Doctor*, King!

ESTELLA CONWILL MAJOZO

**Ms. Recy Taylor,
Gang Rape Survivor
by six White men in Alabama
as she was returning home from church.**

ACT FOUR   SCENE THREE

NIGHT WATCH

ROSA
[HOLDING RED GLOVES.]

Who knew that we would be boycotting this long? They've got to keep the gas tanks full, drop everyone off to their jobs, to the groccry stores, to pay bills, to go to church, to the doctor.

Drivers take tally at night to see if everyone is in, and none of the women are missing.

You know what happened to Miss Recy Taylor.
[RECY TAYLOR STANDS FROM AUDIENCE.]

__ROSA__

I investigated her case for the NAACP. Six White hoodlums took her on the road coming home from church. One after the other they sexually forced themselves on this poor woman. Who can forget that?

__RECY__

The same thing could happen to any one of your wives, mothers, or daughters who forgets, for one instant, that it's best to run, as Miss Alberta says, in bunches.

__ROSA__

When brought before the court, the men claimed she was a whore, a prostitute. Her rape is in the back of every Colored person's mind. A bleeding woman forced to say she liked what they were doing to her.

__RECY__
[STEPS OUT OF AUDIENCE.]

They could have taken their guns and bust my brains out, but the Lord just with me that day.

The Substance Of Things Hoped For

<u>ROSA</u>

Told her, "Act like I do with my husband or I'll cut your damn throat!" They got her in the car and carried her straight through the wood. After they messed over her they said, "We going to take you back. But if you tell it, we'll kill you."

<u>RECY</u>

The people seemed like they wasn't concerned about what happened to me. I have to live through this.

<u>WISDOM</u>

> *Cherished daughter,*
> *God has counted you tossing,*
> *and put your tears in His bottle.*
>
> *He sees, He hears,*
> *He vindicates.*

[ROSA EMBRACES RECY THEN EXITS.]
[RECY SITS.] [WISDOM EXITS.]

**Mrs. Mary McLeod Bethune,
Civil Rights Advocate.
Founder of Bethune-Cookman College.**

ACT FOUR   SCENE FOUR

MOURNING

MOMMA GILMORE
[HOLDS A CHURCH BULLETIN.]

There's a hush over the sanctuary this morning. The church is in mourning. Miss Mary Mcleod Bethune died in her sleep last night. God rest her soul.

We're coming up on two hundred and fifty days. Some babies born in less time than that!

Miss Bethune has been here lots of times from Daytona where she started her college. Lots of our girls go there.

She headed up the woman's organization for the uplift of the race, and even became friends with the first lady, Miss Eleanor Roosevelt.

Like I say, when a mother dies, something taken from the earth that ain't gonna never be again. Something powerful. Something necessary as love.

One day Miss Bethune was invited to the White House for dinner.
[MARY DRESSED IN WHITE ENTERS CLUTCHING AN ENVELOPE.]

The White lady beside her acted like she don't want to sit next to her.

"Uh, are you sitting here?"
She ought to be hoping some of Miss Bethune's shine rub off on her.

Miss Bethune didn't go off on the woman. She kept her dignity.

First Lady Miss Eleanor Roosevelt heard all this rigormoro, and when she found out what it was about, said—

The Substance Of Things Hoped For

MARY

"No problem. Come on up here and sit next to me, Miss Bethune."

MOMMA GILMORE

Ah-ha, *Miss* Bethune!—put the handle on her name. The dingbat who snubbed Miss Bethune sat there with her mouth hanging open for a fly to go in.

Miss Roosevelt and Miss Bethune became friends that very day.

She's got enough sense to know another queen when she sees one.

These words of hers were written in our bulletin.

MARY

"I leave your love. Love builds. It is positive and helpful. It is more beneficial than hate. 'Love thy neighbor' is a precept which could transform the world if it were universally practiced."
[DANCER ENTERS, THEN ESCORTS MARY FROM THE STAGE.]

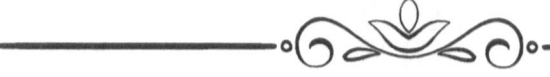

ACT FIVE   SCENE ONE

WHEN KING WAS PRINCE

MOMMA GILMORE

Mark watched Reverend King at the dining table. Reverend King called him over and started talking about when he was Mark's age We're well into winter and he looks like he wants to go somewhere and hibernate. Like I say, it's been three hundred and sixty-five days. That one year mark has everybody looking back.

When he twelve, Reverend King was in a speech contest and his teacher, Miss Sarah Bradley, took him to Dublin, about ninety miles
[SARAH ENTERS HOLDING SATCHEL.]

Anyhow, on the way home, the bus filled up and White folks needed his seat. But after doing his "We're all equal" speech and believing every word of it, he refused to get up. Bus driver came back, looked him in the eye, and called him a bunch of black blasphemies.

Miss Bradley bent down and pleaded with him to get up.

SARAH
[BENDS DOWN OVER HIM.]

Martin, please. We're going have to stand. We have to obey the law.

I look at the stares, the demon faces glaring at the child. *Lord, it's just me and this boy on this far-away bus and he's insisting on something that could leave him dead.*

MOMMA GILMORE

At that moment, I remembered the driver cursing at Miss Rosa, *"Your uppity ass is going to jail!"*

And Miss Coretta going on about her daddy's lumber mill being burned to the ground.

And Miss Mamie asking, *"Have you ever sent a loved son on vacation, and had him returned to you in a pine box?"* Young Martin saw the fright in Miss Sarah's face then reluctantly, by the grace of God, he stood.
[SARAH STANDS.]

Reverend didn't say what made him get up. Just that he rode all ninety miles standing on his feet, and that it was the maddest he had ever been in his life.
[SARAH EXITS.]

The Substance Of Things Hoped For

ACT FIVE SCENE TWO

STILL STANDING

MOMMA GILMORE

The days drag along, no sign of change. Reverend King and his folks are still meeting downtown and holding out with our demands.

Why negotiate? Why give in now? We've pulled all the city's money and made our own way.

They jailed us, drove their cars through our neighborhood harassing us, sent folk out to spy on us, run us through on sidewalks bombed our houses, and look at us—

ESTELLA CONWILL MAJOZO

WISDOM

Still standing.

MOMMA GILMORE

They have killed our children, raped our women, tried to break our souls, but look at us.

WISDOM

Still standing.

MOMMA GILMORE

We just have to hold on a little long, bear down a little harder.

All these pangs are not for naught.

WISDOM

Still standing.

ACT FIVE   SCENE THREE

BIRTH

MOMMA GILMORE

Great God of heaven! It finally happened!

ROSA, CORETTA, AND JO ANN AND MOMMA GILMORE
[ALL ENTER, HUG ONE ANOTHER, AND SPEAK OVER ONE ANOTHER.]

Thank you Jesus!
He's an on time God!
Praise His holy name!"
Glory, Glory!
Won't He do it!

Praise the Lord!

CORETTA

381 days!

MOMMA GILMORE

Segregation on buses is done.

MAMIE
[ENTERS.]

The world is bearing witness!

CLAUDETTE
[ENTERS.]

They got something to see!
[HUGS JO ANN.]

MOMMA GILMORE
[POINTS TO TELEVISION.]

Television stations from all around aiming their cameras at them.

ALBERTA
[ENTERS, POINTS TO TELEVISION.]
There's my dear Martin—

CORETTA
[HUGS ALBERTA.]

And Reverend Shuttlesworth—
Reverend Abernathy, and The Durrs—

CLAUDETTE

The somebodiness Reverend King talked about is right before our eyes!

MOMMA GILMORE

They tried—

CORETTA

They sure did,

MOMMA GILMORE

to appeal but the Supreme Court

ROSA AND CORETTA

upheld the decision.

RECY

[ENTERS.]
All the bearing up—

SARAH

[ENTERS.]

Striving—

VIRGINIA

[ENTERS.]

Riding seven deep in cars from dawn to midnight—
has all been worth it!

MOMMA GILMORE

Lord Jesus, my children and all the children from here to eternity can just keep their seat, Miss Rosa!

JO ANN, MOMMA GILMORE, CORETTA, ALBERTA, MAMIE, CLAUDETTE, SARAH

[INTERMITTENTLY.]

Amen to that,
Praise God!
Go on, girl!
Hallelujah!
Amen!
She did that!

ROSA

SH-H-H, Reverend King's at the mic.

"…I want to give thanks to Almighty God for this victory. We can truly say we have seen truth crucified and goodness buried, but we kept going with the conviction that truth crushed to earth—"

ALL THE CHARACTERS TOGETHER

"Will rise again!"

WISDOM

>*The Great Lord Almighty,*
>*whose Word goes forth upon the earth*
>*and does not return to Him void,*
>*proves the name of this place true.*
>*HA-llelujah!*

ESTELLA CONWILL MAJOZO

Montgomery means
King of the Mountain!

ALL THE CHARACTERS

HA-llelujah!

WISDOM

Our Lord is King here,

ALL CHARACTERS

Praise God!
Amen!
Thank you, Jesus!
He's mighty!

WISDOM

King of this mountain!
King of this nation!
Mighty King over all the earth!

ALL THE CHARACTERS

[DANCER PERFORMS WITH SINGING.]

(SING.)
Just come to praise you

The Substance Of Things Hoped For

<u>*Forever and ever and ever*</u>
   <u>Come on</u>
<u>*For all you've done for me.*</u>
<u>*Blessing and glory and honor*</u>
<u>*They all belong to you.*</u>
   <u>What you say?</u>
<u>*Thank you, Jesus,*</u>
<u>*for blessing me.*</u>

   <u>Get on your feet!</u>
<u>*Just come to praise you*</u>
<u>*Forever and ever and ever*</u>
   <u>Come on now</u>
<u>*For all you've done*</u>
   <u>Yeah, Yeah, Yeah!</u>
<u>*for me.*</u>

<u>*Blessing and glory and honor*</u>
<u>*They all belong to you.*</u>
   <u>What you say?</u>
<u>*Thank you, Jesus,*</u>
<u>*for blessing me.*</u>
   <u>One more time.</u>
<u>*Just come to praise you*</u>
<u>*Forever and ever and ever*</u>

ESTELLA CONWILL MAJOZO

<u>Come on now</u>
<u>*For all you've done*</u>
      <u>Yeah, Yeah, Yeah!</u>
<u>*for me.*</u>

<u>*Blessing and glory and honor*</u>
<u>*They all belong to you.*</u>
<u>*Thank you, Jesus,*</u>
<u>*for blessing me.*</u>
(Maurette Brown Clark)

THE END OF PART ONE.

ESTELLA CONWILL MAJOZO

The Substance of Things Hoped For

THE CONTINUUM

The Substance Of Things Hoped For

CONTENTS
PART TWO

Attorney Dafina Ward

Dr. Patrice Lowe

Mrs. Priscilla Hancock Cooper

Mrs. Teri Melonson

Mrs. Barbara Brown

Mrs. Pam Marcus

Ms. Patty Durbin

Ms. Dixie Cacho

Ms. Rhea Berry

Mrs. Aleida Pleasants

Mrs. Bernice Hatchett

Mrs. Syvenia Davis

Dr. Yalonda JD Green

Mrs. Angelica Hickerson

Dr. Shanna Smith

Mrs. Wanda Fay Darby

Mrs. Claudette McCarter

Sister Patsy Guyton

ESTELLA CONWILL MAJOZO

The contemporary women in this following section, in certain respects, fit the profiles of the historical women of the Montgomery Boycott. They caught the vison and accepted the grace to continue the quest. In the spirit of reverberation, they are the cultural progeny that call future women to don their own mantles.

> Could you be another Rosa Parks,
> the spark that starts the flame?
> Or a Coretta King
> living up to the name?
>
> How about a Jo Ann Robinson
> who heralds the day?
> Could you like Georgia Gilmore
> feed movements of today?
>
> How about a Mamie Till
> turning pain to inspiration?
> Or an Alberta King
> who overcomes trepidation?
>
> Could your song uplift others,
> bring glory to God's name?
> When all about you languish

The Substance Of Things Hoped For

will you share Mahalia's claim?

Will you tell the truth
regardless of the frowns?
Will you like Claudette Colvin
wear your crown?

ESTELLA CONWILL MAJOZO

ATTORNEY DAFINA WARD
Rosa Parks

The Substance Of Things Hoped For

EXAMINING THE LEGALITY OF CUSTOMS AND PRACTICES

Rosa Parks challenged the unjust practices and laws of segregation in her day. She resisted the legal disregard of human rights.

As a lawyer, you work extensively addressing the disparity in the treatment of those living with AIDs and those who are HIV positive in our society. You were recently featured on the nationally televised Jennifer Hudson Show, bringing to light the work that must be done. Describe the challenges faced in the work that you do.

The late Congressman John Lewis once described HIV as the Civil Rights issue of our time because it reveals the systematic health inequities that continue to exist in our day, especially in the south. The NAACP had a map of the US in the early 20th century to show where lynching occurred. If you do an overlay of the current state of our country, the same states that had the most racial violence then now have the highest rates of HIV among Black folk and the greater health disparities. The work I do is very important because if we end HIV in this country we will have ended a significant health injustice.

Dafina Ward is Executive Director of Southern AIDS Coalition. She lives in Bluffton, South Caroline with her family.

*All who are called to enforce
or confront the law,
take to heart and refresh your
spirit with this Bible verse:*

"THEN PETER AND THE APOSTLES ANSWERED, 'WE MUST OBEY GOD RATHER THAN MEN."

ACTS 5:29.

The Substance Of Things Hoped For

DR. PATRICE S. LOWE
Jo Ann Robinson

ESTELLA CONWILL MAJOZO

ASSESSING CONDITIONS AND PROVIDING STRATEGIES FOR ADVANCEMENT

JoAnn Robinson was a professor at Alabama State University during the Montgomery bus boycott. She diagnosed the impediments facing our people and seized the moment to draw up fliers which she distributed throughout the community expressing a remedy for our people's predicament.

You are a diagnostician in Houston, Texas. You test children in the public schools for challenges that may impair them so they can be properly assisted. How important is the work that you do in the progression of our people?

It is important that we are present for our children, demographically, emotionally, socially, and of course academically. Our knowledge of our community, of ourselves as a people, and our ability to distinguish between what has been noted as systematic over-identification verses authentic disability of Black and brown children in special education is imperative. Knowing the difference can make a difference.

In that we are trained, know ourselves, and our communities, we are in prime position to catch the children who might easily fall through the cracks, be ignored, or routed through the pre-school to prison pipeline.

We provide school districts, schools, communities, and families insight on specific needs and support required for students with disabilities. Our service enables students to be self-sufficient, and successful. When we do this, it literally changes lives.

Patrice S. Lowe is a diagnostician who lives with her family in Houston, Texas.

*All who are charged to lead
and analyze any situation
that involves the destiny of others,
take to heart, and refresh your
spirit with this Bible verse:*

*"IF ANY MAN LACKS WISDOM
YOU SHOULD ASK GOD
WHO GIVES GENEROUSLY
TO ALL WITHOUT FINDING
FAULT AND IT WILL BE
GIVEN TO YOU."
JAMES 1:5.*

The Substance Of Things Hoped For

MRS. PRISCILLA HANCOCK COOPER
Coretta Scott King

ESTELLA CONWILL MAJOZO

PRESERVING OUR CULTURAL LEGACIES

One of Coretta Scott King's greatest accomplishment is the preservation of her husband's legacy after his assassination She worked tirelessly to make sure Dr. Martin Luther King, Jr.'s work was rightfully recognized and his legacy perpetuated.

Your work after leaving the Birmingham Civil Rights Institute has been with the Alabama African American Civil Rights Heritage Site Consortium, preserving the cultural history of twenty Civil Rights sites in Birmingham, Mongomery, Selma and the Black Belt.. Talk a bit about the importance of such work.

The preservation of the Civil Rights sites is actually preservation and protection of our history. The power of those places is that they are the visible and physical manifestation of a legacy and stories too often forgotten or untold. The Civil Right movement is part of the continuum of the African American struggle for freedom and self-determination.

The Substance Of Things Hoped For

Too often, the events of the 1950s and 1960w are taken out of context. Theses instructions trace the beginnings of the end of the Civil War and the aftermath of Reconstruction.

Not only were they the centers and safe havens to the Civil Rights Movement, but they were the institutions that created and supported Black self-sufficiency by developing at their center for education, businesses and social service and cultural expression.

Understanding this history and this legacy empowers this generation to know its ability and responsibility to create positive change. We are challenged to make it happen.

Priscilla Hancock Cooper is the retired founding director of the Alabama African American Civil Rights Consortium, Inc. She resides in Birmingham, Alabama.

*All who are in the role of wife,
nurturer, or legacy builder,
take to heart and refresh your spirit
with this Bible verse:*

'LET LOVE

AND FAITHFULESS

NEVER LEAVE YOU,

BIND THEM

AROUND YOUR NECK,

WRITE THEM ON THE TABLET

OF YOUR HEART."

PROVERBS 3:3-4.

The Substance Of Things Hoped For

MRS. TERI MELONSON
Georgia Gilmore

ADDRESSING WOMEN'S HEALTH ISSUES

Georgia Gilmore was a midwife of the Montgomery community who tended women bringing forth new life—a situation that could be stressful and traumatizing at time.

You are a registered nurse who has been recognized by the medical professions for your techniques in alleviating anxiety in surgery patients. Would you explain some of those techniques you employ?

I attended patients who were undergoing surgery and helped with their pain control. I was recognized by MD Anderson Hospital with the outstanding nurse award. Out of 10,000 nurses, I was acknowledged for outstanding service. I was on the team who placed an epidermal catheter for post operative pain control. We would meet the patient and the catheter would be placed, and after surgery I would monitor it. Many times, I would make rounds and let patients know that I would make sure that their pain would be controlled. There were many steps to this. I would give then an extra dose of medicine and make sure that it was working. If it wasn't working, I would call the doctor and he would give them more medicine and check to see if the catheter had not dislodged.

Much of the care has to do with monitoring and being in touch with patients, listening to their disclosures, and assuring them that they are getting the best possible care.

Historically, Black women were believed by the medical profession to not experience pain as the White counterparts—an underlying assumption held by many who treat Black women today. This causes maltreatment of women postnatally. You must listen; you must assure your patients and work with them. This is my charge, my spiritual charge.

Teri Melonson is a retired nurse who lives with her husband in Houston, Texas.

*All who are in the role
of healer or caretaker of any sort,
take to heart
and refresh your spirit
with this Bible verse.*

"COME UNTO ME ALL

WHO ARE WEARY

AND HEAVY BURDENED

AND I WILL GIVE YOU REST."

MATTHEW 11:28-29.

The Substance Of Things Hoped For

MS. BABBARA BROWN
Mamie Till

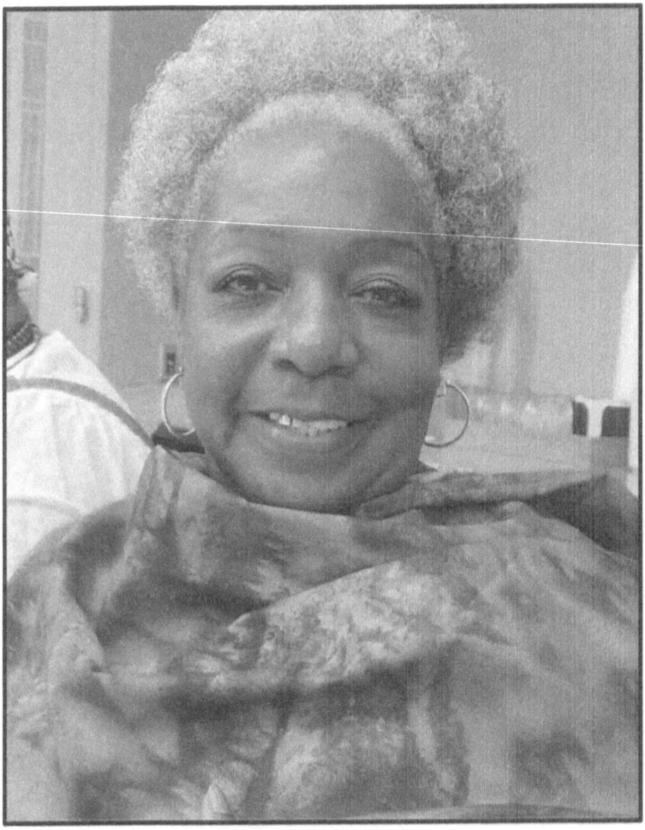

ESTELLA CONWILL MAJOZO

FACING VIOLENCE IN THE COMMUNITY

Mamie Till suffered the horrific death of her son, Emmit, at the hands of brutal White men in Mississippi. She held his funeral with an open casket because she wanted the world to see what they did to her son.

You experienced brutality against your son at the hands of another Black man. Will you speak about this atrocity that happens too frequently in the Black community?

My son got shot eight times and didn't die. He was at a club and it was a case of mistaken identity. The shooter thought he was someone else and said, "Nigger, you going to die tonight." He shot him point black eight times. My son said, "Momma I could see the smoke and flashes from the gun. And smell the powder."

Violence from the outside is bad, but this kind of Black-on-Black violence is abominable. Where does it come from? From the type of home the young man was brought up in; the kind of anger he carried. He said at the trial he mistakenly thought that he was encountering someone who had done something to him earlier that evening. He meant to kill him. The mercies of God spared my son.

The Substance Of Things Hoped For

What can we do to prevent things like this? We have to intervene when our kids are young and are programmed like this with hurt, pain, anger, and hunger. The community let him down. Intervention could have saved him. Maybe a mean, a hug, or a conversation. I forgave the boy. It took a minute. He's got a mother too and he is a child of God.

A copper penny caught the death bullet that was meant for his heart. The surgeon came out with the penny all snarled with gunpowder and wiped away blood. He said, "if your son does not believe in God, he needs to. This penny saved his life."

I had just given my life back to God and was at church upholstering and following His divine will when I got the word. On my way to the hospital, I couldn't say anything. I just called His name. Jesus. They stopped my car and told me that my son was dead, and I cried out, The devil is a liar! Yes, Lord.

Barbara Brown is a U.S. Army veteran who lives in Houston, Texas by way of Des Moines, Iowa.

ESTELLA CONWILL MAJOZO

All who have suffered
from the murder or violence
to a loved-one
take to heart
and refresh your spirit
with this Bible verse:

"BELOVED,

NEVER AVENGE YOURSELVES,

BUT LEAVE IT

TO THE WRATH OF GOD,

FOR IT IS WRITTEN,

'VENGEANCE IS MINE,

I WILL REPAY, SAYS THE LORD.' "

ROMANS 12:19.

The Substance Of Things Hoped For

MRS. PAM MARCUS
Sarah Bradley

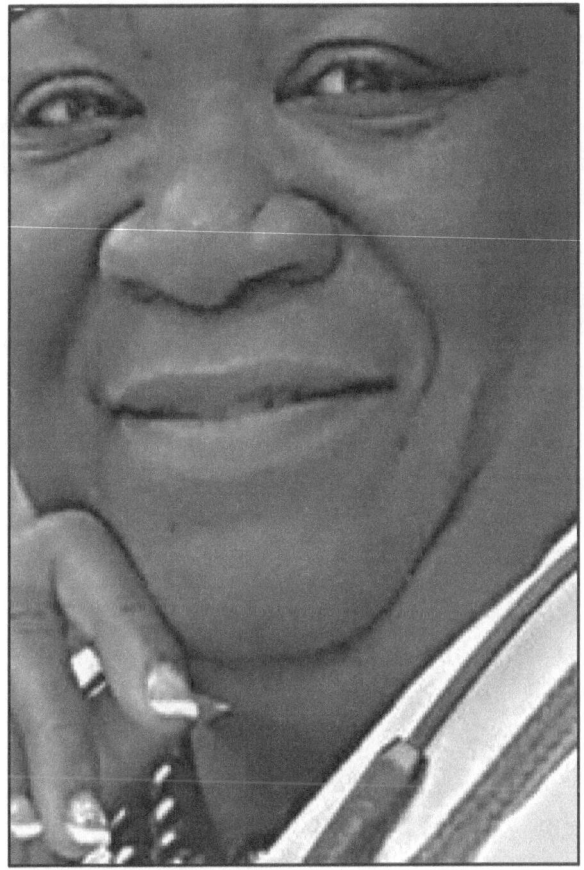

ESTELLA CONWILL MAJOZO

ENCOURAGING ZEAL WHILE INSTILLING SURVIVAL SKILLS IN OUR YOUTH

Martin Luther King, Jr., as a child, felt the impulse to resist the injustice he experienced while riding home on a public bus from a neighboring town in Georgia. He has just won a speech contest where he brilliantly expressed his hope for equality between the races and he would not relent on what he had just presented. His teacher, Sarah Bradley, fought to get him to relinquish his seat on a segregated bus. He eventually obeyed but he said that this was the angriest he had been in his life.

You have been an assistant principal in the Chicago public schools for inner city children who faced discrimination and injustice every day. How do you encourage their zeal to fight against injustice and at the same time teach them to protect themselves against the forces they face?

First of all, keep the zeal. Think about what was done for us in the past. Know that you have a voice. Always keep education at the forefront. Read books, search the internet, get knowledge to move forward. Yes, there are going to be times when you come against opposition but keep God at the forefront. Read His Word to help with the opposition .

When you protest, don't do it by yourselves. Try not to be like Claudette Colvin. Rosa Parks had the NAACP behind her. There are times when you have to move alone. But for the most part, get support. Travel in circles that have the same ideas and ideals as you do. That's what Martin Luther King, Jr. did. He was an individual, but he had many who stood with him. There is might in numbers. They have a cause but others also have that cause.

Knowing the law helps. Don't just pop off. You have to develop discernment.

Pam Marcus is a retired assistant principal from the Chicago public school system, living in Houston, Texas.

All who are charged to teach in any capacity, take to heart and refresh your spirit with this Bible verse:

"TRUST IN THE LORD WITH ALL YOUR HEART AND LEAN NOT UNTO YOUR OWN UNDERSTANDING. IN ALL YOUR WAUS ACKOWEDGE HIM AND HE WIL DIRECT YOUR PATH." PROVERBS 3:5-6.

The Substance Of Things Hoped For

MS. PATTY DURBIN
Jeannie Graetz

ESTELLA CONWILL MAJOZO

CROSSING RACIAL BARRIERS
FOR JUSTICE

Jeannie Graetz was a White woman in Montgomery who aligned herself with the purpose of the boycott. She openly crossed cultural lines to identify with those who were fighting to end segregation on the buses.

You have been associated with circles that cross racial barriers. How important is this in your line of work and in general?

I think it's necessary. There are people who align themselves with what is right; not what is safe, but what is the right thing to do. God's people will do that. It's not a lot of them. People are fearful of losing their identities and the opinions of others stop them. God's people do not care about that. He calls you into hard places. And those places are all identity places. That's what He's doing in all of our lives. Causing us to look at how we define ourselves and how He defines us.

It's not about crossing the line. It's about alignment against something that's not right. I've been dealing with this for two years at work. It's not racism but ageism, but it's all

The Substance Of Things Hoped For

ism. God created genetic codes when He created race at the tower of Babel. He gave them different languages and He separated them. It used to be one big place, after Noah, the people groups of different languages were separated physically and they carried different genetic codes. That's where different races came forth. God created different races, not racism. He loves diversity.

I grew up in rural Kentucky, and they didn't know people of other races. They are very isolated. They are separated and they like it. I was looking for a group of artists that were more diverse. It was only with the art crowd that I met people who thought outside the box. We co-mingled, looked into constructs of Louisville, Kentucky, and established friendships. It moved us into alignment.

After leaving and living in Seattle, living back in Kentucky was very constraining. It felt like a tight pace where I didn't belong. I stretched and hopefully impacted my community. It you can't name the place in Kentucky that you grew up and high school you went to, you were not accepted. It's more than racism. It's place-ism. But God calls us to go, maybe not geographically, but go!

Pattie Durbin works and lives in Denver, Colorado.

ESTELLA CONWILL MAJOZO

All who are in the capacity
of activist,
take to heart
and refresh your spirit
with this Bible verse:
"DO JUSTICE

AND RIGHTEOUSNESS.

AND DELIVER THE ONE

WHO HAS BEEN ROBBED

FROM THE POWER

OF THE OPPRESED."

JEREMIAH 22:3.

The Substance Of Things Hoped For

MS. DIXIE CACHO
Recy Taylor

CONFRONTING SEXUAL VIOLENCE

Recy Taylor was a survivor of violence through rape by six White men who attacked her on the road in Montgomery, Alabama while on her way home from church. The crime was buried and she was left to suffer alone in silence and without accountability.

You are a dancer whose body is her instrument for creative expression and the means of your livelihood. But more than that, you are a human being deserving of respect. You were brutally assaulted by your fiancée and hospitalized for your afflictions. But you were not silent. You identified your assailant, had him arrested and he served time in prison as a result. How important is it that assaulted women fight back by coming to voice and taking back their power?

It is important to come to voice and take back your power after an incident of violence. If not, you are giving your power to your assailant and allowing that to happen to another woman. By speaking out, you are getting your power back. You are empowering yourself. And there is healing in that.

The Substance Of Things Hoped For

It is hard to speak out at first, because you feel shame of being in the position of being assaulted, and you feel ashamed of putting yourself in that position to be assaulted.

There is also the fear that after the assailant is released from prison he may attack you again. But speaking the truth and telling my story, I am able to encourage other women in that same position.

Dixie Cacho is as Belizean dancer and choreographer who lives in Louisville, Kentucky.

*All who are
the survivors of violence,
take to heart
and refresh your spirit
with this Bible verse:*

"THE LORD IS

A REFUGE

FOR THE OPPRESSED,

A STRONGHOD IN TIMES

OF TROUBLE."

PSALM 9:9.

The Substance Of Things Hoped For

MS. RHEA BERRY
Recy Taylor

ESTELLA CONWILL MAJOZO

CONFRONTING SEXUAL VIOLENCE

Recy Taylor was the survivor of violence through rape by five White men who attacked her on the road in Montgomery, Alabama while on her way home from church.

Your situation was different. You at the time were a drug addict and prostituted to support your habit. You were raped and violated five different times in the process. Can you talk a little bit about that abuse and your struggle to pull out in a lineup of six guys, the one who raped you. And how this helped you in your struggle to be free from addiction and prostitution.

One trick picked me up and drove me out to Fort Knox, raped me, and left me there. Another guy tried to kidnap me and I threw his car into park while he was driving. We were riding around, getting high, and he took me down to the flood gates in Portland area in west Louisville, and he raped me in the car. But somebody told the police about it, and a detective found m in the projects getting high.

She showed me pictures of guys. He was there in the lineup. I pointed him out, and asked her how she knew about all this? She told me he was a known rapist.

The Substance Of Things Hoped For

That made me feel like was not alone and that I did matter. And that incident inspired me to start to pull out of this life. This one guy put a gun to my head. And I got busy. My life was threatened right there. I came to realize my life could end right there. My life was not in my hands. I had to learn to act right. Nobody could lay crack in front of me and tell me to do whatever for it. But they could force themselves on me as I was in that predicament.

When you're out there you don't think of the consequences, you've got to think fast. Throw the car in park, jump out, because nothing's worth somebody violating you. That was the beginning of my wake up call, and my forgiveness. God's and my own.

Rhea Berry is a retired federal officer for Transportation Security Administration in Louisville, Kentucky

All who are
the survivors of violence,
take to heart
and refresh your spirit
with this Bible verse:

"THE LORD IS

A REFUGE

FOR THE OPPRESSED,

A STRONGHOD IN TIMES

OF TROUBLE."

PSALM 9:9.

The Substance Of Things Hoped For

MRS. ALEIDA PLAEASANTS
Alberta King

ESTELLA CONWILL MAJOZO

FUNCTIONING AS AN ELDER

Alberta King was the matriarch of the King family. She, indeed, was the counselor and sustainer.

You have been an educator for decades in the Louisville, Kentucky public school system teaching children in the preliminary stages of their development. How important is it that you continue to teach in your community after your retirement? Speak about your role as an elder in the survival of family and community.

———————

There are so many psychological and mental issues that are coming forth in the children. So much fighting and destruction. That's why they kill each other like they do. They are at war with one other. They are still saying this mess that "I'm not going to live till I'm 18." I tell them you are messing up our gene pool. You keep killing the boys off. With the males gone, they few who are left will be the father of these babies. There is not enough diversity. You're going back to slave times. You end up having cousins mating, and brother and sister mating, because you don't know who the fathers are. God did not send you to this earth to die before 18. He sent you with a body that had a certain life expectancy.

I used to sit on the grass with them in the neighborhood and talk. Some of the ones who I had taught earlier. And you hope it gets through.

I got that from my grandfather. They used to watch who was with who, and who were the children who came from those relationships. And they always made sure the children knew who they were related to. It was like keeping their genealogy.

Alieda Pleasant is a retired elementary school teacher who resides in Louisville, Kentucky.

*All who are in the role
of elder, or advisor,
take to heart
and refresh your spirit
with this Bible verse:*

*"PAY CAREFUL ATTENTION
TO YOURSELVES AND TO ALL
THE FLOCK IN WHICH THE HOLY
SPIRIT HAD HADE YOU OVERSEERS,
TO CARE FOR THE CHURCH OF
GOD IN WHICH HE OBTAINED
WITH HIS OWN BLOOD."
ACTS 20:28.*

The Substance Of Things Hoped For

MRS. BERNICE HATCHETT
Alberta King

ESTELLA CONWILL MAJOZO

ACCEPTING THE SOMETIMES DIFFICULT ROLE OF MATRIARCH

Alberta King was a counselor and matriarch of her family, giving advice and direction that benefited generations.

You are from a large extended family. What direction would you give to women who hold the position of matriarch of their family?

I am the oldest of ten children, and I am black sheep of the family. Everybody looks to me for advice. I can't tell them I have any illnesses. I am the one who tends them. When all five of my sisters are together and people see how we interact, they ask me how do you maintain these one way relationships. I don't put myself on a pedestal. I just do what I do. I have lived a blessed life. Even when I was a child and my family needed Christmas presents from the Catholic church, I gave the presents I received to my younger siblings. They didn't know it. When I do things I don't even mention it.

Once, as a young woman, I was in my apartment crying and my mother came by. She was genuinely surprised,

The Substance Of Things Hoped For

"I thought you were the strongest one in the family. The way I raised you, you were supposed to be the strongest one."

There are many sides to being the matriarch. You have to brace up. You have to lead.

Bernice Hatchett lives near her extended family in Houston, Texas.

All who are in the role
of elder,
take to heart
and refresh your spirit
with this Bible verse:

"PAY CAREFUL ATTENTION TO YOURSELVES AND TO ALL THE FLOCK IN WHICH THE HOLY SPIRIT HAD MADE YOU OVERSEERS, TO CARE FOR THE CHURCH OF GOD IN WHICH HE OBTAINED WITH HIS OWN BLOOD."
ACTS 20:28.

The Substance Of Things Hoped For

MRS. SYVENIA DAVIS
Claudette Colvin

DEFENDING THE RIGHT
TO CULTURALLY EXPRESS ONESELF

Even before Rosa Parks, Claudette Colvin held her own protect against injustice by refusing to give up her seat on a segregated Montogomery bus. Her protest was not covered by the media or heralded by her community. Yet it advanced the imperative of acting against injustice. Earlier in high school she decided to wear her hair in a natural style and was ostracized by her fellow students for doing so.

You had a comparable situation as an adult in your workplace in California. Tell us about your resistance and insistence on embracing your own standard of beauty as a Black woman.

My mother always told me when I was growing up to stand up for myself. She believed that if we let people shove us down we would never go anywhere. So when the hair issue came up I was really infuriated. I just had a little bob natural. My hair was not just curly, it was natural.

I really don't remember exactly what the supervisor said. He just hinted that people shouldn't wear their hair like that to work. Of course He didn't let anyone else hear this. Just me. He could have gotten corrected and punished if he did. He would never say his remarks in the open. I had to really go home and pray because in my early days I was a person who just cursed people out without a second thought.

My mother always told me that was not the right way to do things. So I went home and prayed. Lord help me to be able to deal with this the right way.

So I came back work and told him I needed a meeting with him. So we met. I had written down my thoughts so I wouldn't say the wrong thing. I told him that we all had the right to wear our hair any way we wanted, and that if he couldn't accept that I would get a lawyer. I added, please don't say that to me again.

I was bluffing, but it worked. I didn't really have money to get a lawyer. The only lawyer I had was Jesus!

Syvenia Davis is retired and lives in Walnut Creek, California.

The Substance Of Things Hoped For

> *All who are in the role*
> *of activist,*
> *take to heart*
> *and refresh your spirit*
> *with this Bible verse:*
>
> *"BEHOLD*
> *I AM DOING A NEW THING,*
> *NOW IT SPRINGS FORTH,*
> *DO YOU NOT*
> *PERCIEVE IT?"*
> *ISAIAH 43:19.*

ESTELLA CONWILL MAJOZO

DR. YALONDA JD GREEN
Mahalia Jackson

The Substance Of Things Hoped For

USING ART AS A WEAPON

The great Mahlia Jackson one said before going on to the stage, "Get out of the way, Mahalia's about the fight demons!"

You are a singer, poet, and scholar/librarian at the University of Delaware. In what ways does the work that you do as a conscious artist help to combat the real evils that plague our society?

Recognize that the tools and the weapons and the entities that we fight against are often invisible. And the tools, weapons, and instruments with which we fight are also invisible. They are real and they are powerful. And the way we use our voices determine the progress we make.

What comes from inside of us when we sing is a supernatural power that grows from the spark of creation that is unlocked in us. And that makes all things possible. It assures us that the impossibility is possible.

Yalonda JD Green works as a librarian and the University of Delaware and is also a poet/ jazz vocalist.

All who are gifted
with creativity in any capacity,
take to heart
and refresh your spirit
with this Bible verse:

"SING TO THE LORD
A NEW SONG.
SING TO THE LORD, PRAISE
HIS NAME
PROCLAIM HIS SALVATION
DAY AFTER DAY."
PSALM 96: 1-2.

The Substance Of Things Hoped For

MRS. ANGELICA HICKERSON
Mahalia Jackson

ESTELLA CONWILL MAJOZO

TRANSFORMING SELF AND COMMUNITY THROUGH ART

Mahalia Jackson was a great singer who sang in churches and music halls around the world. In the work, Spirit and Blood, we see her having a profound effect on Reverend Martin Luther King, Jr., and the Montgomery bus boycott.

You are a singer/songwriter. Talk about the function of your art in transforming society.

The function and purpose of my art is exemplified in a song that I have written.

> Bury me in the tomb,
> I got be made new,
> Seraphim, roll my stone,
> there's new flesh on dry bone.

It's a personal choice. It's not a journey that's convenient, but it yields great reward if we are persistent. I think it helps people to understand and not fear that process, but to see it with hope.

The Substance Of Things Hoped For

I compose and sing with my husband, a musician. It's just work that we do. It's normal. We create a lot of things together. I don't see it any different from cleaning the kitchen together, folding towels together. I'm accustomed to working with him. It doesn't

feel any less great than washing dishes together. We are praising God. It's my assignment.

Angelica Hickerson is an educator and a singer/songwriter who lives with her family in Houston, Texas.

ESTELLA CONWILL MAJOZO

All who are singers
of praise-songs,
take to heart
and refresh your spirit
with this Bible verse:

"I WILL SING

OF YOUR STRENGTH."

PSALM 59:16.

The Substance Of Things Hoped For

DR. SHANNA L. SMITH
Mary McLeod Bethune

ESTELLA CONWILL MAJOZO

MAINTAINING THE INTEGRITY OF HISTORICALLY BLACK COLLEGES AND UNIVERSITIES

Mary McLeod Bethune founded Bethune College, a Historically Black College and University (HBCU) for girls in Daytona Beach, Florida at the start of the century. She spoke in Montogomery several times during her lifetime.

You teach literature at Jackson State University, an HBCU. How important is it that Historically Black Colleges and Universities remain vibrant and relevant in the 21st century? What do Black universities offer that is uniquely beneficial to students?

―――――― ――――――

HBCUs provide for Black young adults in particular a space of welcome, a space of challenge, a space of preparation, a space of mentorship, a space of correction and redirection. And finally, a space for guidance, opportunity, and celebration.

We know that we do get some of the best and talented, and also those who can be the best if tended. We have to develop the skills and sometimes they have to fail forward. Sometimes they mess us. But what we don't do is give up.

When I was at Kentucky State University, another historically Black university as a student I had people who didn't give up on me. Who gave me a change to mature. I pass it forward. It allows you to be in your imperfect state.

The PWIs (predominant White Institutions) might recruit you and take your money, but they will also easily show you the door. We allow you to try, repeat, assess, and go on to succeed.

Shanna L Smith is an associate professor at Jackson State University in Mississippi.

All who are teachers
in higher learning,
take to heart
and refresh your spirit
with this Bible verse:

"AND THEY WERE ALL
TAUGHT
BY GOD."
ISAIAH 54:13.

The Substance Of Things Hoped For

MRS. WANDA FAY DARBY
Georgia Gilmore

ESTELLA CONWILL MAJOZO

SUSTAINING ECONOMICAL SUPPORT IN CULTURAL COMMUITIES

Georgia Gilmore was a woman of many talents, one of which was her culinary contributions to the Montgomery bus boycott. In fact, Dr. Martin Luther King, Jr. said that the boycott would not have been possible with her.

You also are a woman of many talents—a businesswoman, a professional seamstress, and a Louisiana chef whose craft you derived from your mother and grandmother. Tell us a bit about the function of food as a cultural means of solidarity and survival in our community.

Food brought us together from all over. My mother would cook for people who didn't have food in the neighborhood. She would cook a lot of food to raise money so people could pay their bills. Sometimes people couldn't pay rent. We would a have a waist-line party—whatever measurement your waistline was, that's how much you would pay to eat. And the money would go towards that family.

My mother had a whole wing of the church built by selling sweet dough pies. She always cared for people like that.

The Substance Of Things Hoped For

Just to see the people's happy faces was inspiring. I would go with her sometimes to strip malls and sell pies like the girls sell girl scout cookies.

She would make red beans and rice, and cornbread, or she would buy a case of catfish and make catfish dinners. Or she'd buy the chicken leg quarters and we'd make dinners. They were excellent. My dad whenever he wasn't working would barbe-be-que. We would run out every time. That's how the community was sustained. We didn't have homeless people. I never saw my first homeless person until I moved to California.

I would always ask the homeless, after I acknowledged them, why are you homeless? So that's how I came to help the homeless in the Oakland Bay area. My daughter did the same thing.

Wanda Faye Darby lives in Houston, Texas by way of California and Eunice, Louisiana.

*All who provide food for others
as farmers, dieticians, or cooks,
take to heart
and refresh your spirit
with this Bible verse:*

"AND IF YOU SPEND YOURSELF IN BEHALF OF THE HUNGRY, AND SATISFY THE NEEDS OF THE OPPRESSED, THEN YOUR LIGHT WILL RISE IN THE DARKNESS, AND YOU NIGHT WILL BECOME LIKE THE NOONDAY."

ISAIAH 58:10.

The Substance Of Things Hoped For

MRS. CLAUDETTE MCCARTER
Sojourner Truth

ESTELLA CONWILL MAJOZO

INTERCEDING
AS A MEANS OF COMMNITY SURVIVAL

Sojourner Truth was one of the ancestors who held Claudette Colvin in the segregated seat in the Montgomery bus. That contributed to the people's understanding that they must resist oppression.

You are not an ancestor but a spirit-filled women who is an intercessor for others. How necessary is it for a true intercessor to stay in the presence of the Lord for her words to have power?

You go to God with a sincere heart and it doesn't take long for Him to act. Right now, it's much that He's getting his people ready for. All the miracles that He prophesied to me He is getting ready to overflow. It's going to happen just like anything else. The longer you stay on the job, the higher promotion you get. That's the same way with God. You've got that relationship with Him. When you go to Him, He obliges. We've got that connection. That's all that matters.

That's the reason He chooses us. He has put compassion and love in our hearts so we can go in and move mountains. Intercessors have to stay in His presence and stay prayed up. You might have to suffer some but trust in God, and He will come though. Look at Martin Luther King. He believed that

God was going to break this separation. We would have still been going through segregation. He believed in God. He had that relationship. It matters. Pray, child, Pray.

Claudette McCarter is an evangelist who lives in Houston, Texas.

*All who are intercessors
take to heart
and refresh your spirit
with this Bible verse:*

"GOD IS OUR REFUGE

AND OUR STRETNGTH.

IN HIM DO WE TRUST"

PSALM 91.

The Substance Of Things Hoped For

SISTER PATSY GUYTON
Harriet Tubman

ESTELLA CONWILL MAJOZO

FORTIFYING COMMUNITY THROUGH PRAYER

Harriet Tubman was one of the two ancestors who held Claudette Colvin in her segregated seat on the Montgomery bus so that she could not get up. She was, in fact, the enforcer, a conductor for freedom, a conduit of grace.

You are an intercessor who prays for family, community, and the world. How necessary is it that we have intercessors who push and believe in the transformative power of God?

The gift of an intercessor is powerful. God asks us to pray for one another that we may be healed. The greatest intercessor, of course. was Jesus Christ. Throughout scripture God has us uplifting one another. Moses had armorbearers, When I think of intercessors, three come to mind, Jesus Christ, my grandfather, and the Blessed Mother of Jesus. They prayed unceasingly and we are reaping the benefits of their seed. Our healing in mind, soul, and spirit, and even the deliverance from slavery, being able to live through Jim Crow, segregation, all the things we have had to go through and still have to go through just because of the color of our skin were accomplished by intercessory prayer. There were loved ones who interceded on our behalf.

There is a song that goes, "*My momma pray for me/ had me on her mind/ took a little time to pray for me/ I'm so glad she prayed/ I'm so glad she prayed/, I'm so glad she prayed for me.*"

We have to pray to God for one another. As part of the mystical body of Christ, we are called to do so.

Sister Patsy Guyton is a religious nun who lives in Montogomery, Alabama, the historic site of this project.

*All who are intercessors
take to heart
and refresh your spirit
with this Bible verse:*

"MAY THE LORD BLESS

YOU AND KEEP YOU.

MAY HE MAKE HIS FACE

SHINE UPON YOU

AND BE GRACIOUS

UNTO YOU."

NUMBERS 6:24-26.

DR. ESTELLA CONWILL MAJOZO
Author of *The Substance of Things Hoped For*

COMMENTARY

I am grateful for all the historical women who lived the meanings of their names, and for the contemporary women who share their experiences in this book and continue the work that must be done.

The people coming behind us will not personally know Rosa Parks, Coretta King, Georgia Gilmore, Jo Ann Robinson, and Mamie Till. They may not have even heard of some of the contemporary women featured in this work. But they know *you*.

They know the nurses, doulas, and healers who control the physical pain they endure. They know the advocates, social scientists and teachers who preserve our history. They know the ones who fight for change in the legal system, and those who intercede for them. They know the benefits wrought from *your* efforts and the impact *you* make in their lives And knowing you, they will, hopefully pass these gifts on to people in their lives who need compassion, guidance and healing

The blessings of the Lord are passed from person to person and they take us from glory to glory. Never think that your efforts are thrown to the wind. The Holy Spirit of God ignites in us the power to break every chain that hinders us from true freedom. That's why the scriptural captions end each section. They are an invitation for you to see aspects of yourself in the profiles of these women.

God is forever drawing circles upon the deep, creating communities that incite transformation. And He sends the spirit of Wisdom to inspire us. As the Word of Our Lord tells us, "Whoever gets up early to seek her, will find her, sitting at the door."

Estella Conwill Majozo is a poet, retired professor, performance artist, and guide for developing spiritually. She resides in Houston, Texas.

The Substance Of Things Hoped For

The End

www.ingramcontent.com/pod-product-compliance
Lightning Source LLC
Chambersburg PA
CBHW022104160426
43198CB00008B/341